The B.Y.T.C.H. BOOK

Building Your Trojan Creative Horse

This book attributes to taking the fear out of being an entrepreneur through the eyes of the author.

Dawn Michelle Williams

IAmDawnWilliams.com

The B.Y.T.C.H. book

by Dawn Michelle Williams

Copyright © 2021 Da Crankin Shop LLC, The Research Departments

All rights reserved.

For bookings, classes, retail items and more please visit:

www.IAmDawnWilliams.com

The B.Y.T.C.H. Book™

(Building Your Trojan Creative Horse)

We all are familiar with the story of the trojan horse. If you aren't, let me shorten it for you. It's about Greek soldiers who, after a period of time, were able to win a war by using a certain tactic. They hid the soldiers in a wooden horse in order to transport themselves to the other side. This book matches experiences with entrepreneurship with actual lessons learned.

Each genre of entrepreneurship has similar obstacles. Most often, it's other people who desire to stop you. This book is a tool to help you build your proverbial "Trojan Horse" to assist your path to success as an entrepreneur.

Edited by Cristina Finan Alonso

Published by The Research Departments™

Table of Contents

Dedication

This book is dedicated to my husband and children. The occurrence of tragedy can either make or break you. Preparing for the death of someone is nearly impossible. It's preparing for the trauma AFTER that is detrimental. The death of my daddy in 2020 in part fuels my motivation for business. It's bigger than money. It's the ability to see someone else's trauma, knowing you have the tools to show them how to move on before they ever do.

My beautiful children: I never thought I could ever love anyone more than I love myself until you both came. It (creation) was written by Allah for you to teach me about myself in order to cease generational mistakes.

(Big) Umar: The way Allah put us in each other's path is astounding. You are the definition of tough love. You are the friend who tells the truth no matter how much it hurts, the one who is always there, especially during tragedy. My favorite quote you ever said to me is, "Life is hard. Get over it. What's the next move." You keep me moving past tragedy. The therapist without the degree.

Chapter 1
The Geriatric Psycho

Being an entrepreneur is similar to jumping out of a plane and building a parachute on the way down. It is chaotic, and you always are expected to have the appearance that you have it all together regardless of the circumstances.

The commercial landlord from hell sparked the entrepreneurial hustle in me once again. The difference was that this time (2016), I had a strong support system. Fifteen years prior, I was a complete disaster. It was the summer prior to the infamous U.S. election of Trump v. Clinton. Before the winner was to be announced in November, my husband and I had already predicted Trump was going to win. We weren't sure if him being president would be tragic or wonderful, especially looking at all dynamics of the proverbial skeletons on each side. What we knew for certain was that since he was about to win, we needed to prepare to embark upon something monumental that would secure our financial future. At that time, I was the salon manager at a nursing home. Because I was hooking these elderly ladies up with gorgeous styles, a clientele came in a matter of a few years. So, when this preparation was met with opportunity, a quick google search produced an available retail location for a future salon.

I immediately searched for a retail location. We met with a very professional realtor. I remember he kept rushing me to read the lease. I was new to the game, and he knew it. I rushed through it, not questioning any terms (in which some were outrageous). I remember as I signed the last line, he started laughing while saying how the landlord "gets on his nerves" because she is very "picky". I was taken aback because it is highly unusual in the business world to disclose such personal grievances with someone you don't know (red flag #1).

The day of the exchange of keys, the landlord (the geriatric psycho) rescheduled a few times prior. I remember she settled on a late afternoon time after 12. I was taken aback again when she walked through the door late and fumbled through the keys alleging she didn't have all of them (red flag #2). We looked at the property on July 8th, paid her a deposit of $3600 on the 28th, and she still "couldn't find a key" on August 1st…AFTER 12 pm? I stood there with my two children (then 8 and 10 years old) waiting. I KNEW on first eye contact that our souls did not match. She looked at me in disgust.

When I walked into the lease space, I noticed a large red sectional couch in the 750 square foot suite. When I asked her when it would be moved, she snapped at me. This chick was in her 70's. I stood in shock from the arrogance she displayed. She left, and at that point, I didn't care about her attitude. It took her a week or so to remove it.

The next 30 days were a disaster. I thought renting a brick and mortar would be hard due to government licensing requirements. No! All of the government employees (county, state, and federal) were polite and made their expectations clear. My battle was only with the geriatric psycho. By the time I held my grand opening, we had already had an altercation. It was like a geriatric reality show (which I was used to from working at a nursing home). Long story short, this landlord lived two doors down from the building. I found out after signing the lease that she had a business upstairs (a METHADONE clinic). So, she had an arrangement with the local post office to divert mail from the commercial building to her house. She then would distribute mail to the tenants at her leisure (which was about once or twice a week). To add insult to injury, she actually opened tenants' mail PRIOR to delivering it. I had an assistant who witnessed it and photographed the act.

When I showed my cotenant the picture of her opening the mail, he stood frozen in a fear-like state. He literally accepted this behavior. Anyway, I asked the post office for a key to the cluster mailbox. They gave me the runaround, even stating they had no idea where Eastern Avenue was. The post office was five minutes away. I was astounded by the corruption. I called a locksmith to drill the mailbox open and make me a key. Oh my goodness gracious. First, a methadone clinic employee came down the stairs in silence. I was stuck. Then, this heffa comes flying out of her house…on foot…in a trench coat...in August…with her pajamas under the coat. Yes, read that again. This lady was a self-described "socialite" on social media platforms behaving like a reality star. She threw the locksmith's toolbox across the lawn while cursing at me and him. At that point, I called my husband, who was in the salon painting. Side note: I always attract psychopathic bullies like this. I needed my husband to see this because it's hard for him to imagine the chaos I describe unless he is there. Hunny baby, once this lady mentioned my son, all bets were off. I let her have it (verbally, of course). That was the first altercation (I got my mailbox key, though).

The second altercation

The HVAC system. Hunny BAYBAYYYY. Prince George's County Maryland regulations mandate a ventilation system for salons. The geriatric psycho told me I couldn't put up a ventilation system because I'd have to cut through an exterior wall. We come to find out that the ventilation system was all screwed up in the building. So, on one hand the lease required me to be fully licensed and operational within 90 days (although the other businesses within the building were not all in compliance, but I shall digress). Then, on the other hand, she cited a violation of her request (to not drill a hole in the wall) as grounds for eviction. It was a catch-22. I contacted a family friend who referred me to a gracious lawyer who offered me advice. Lesson #1: law supersedes any leasing requirement. Obey the law first. So, the HVAC system went up, and all heck broke loose.

The landlord managed to pull a county official in to force the removal of the HVAC system, citing that it was illegal. I was so terrified. I couldn't function because I was hung up on the fact that "she didn't like me. The official ended up leaving because his hands were tied. The HVAC system was legally installed by my nephew.

During the illegal inspection, I was in such a state of anger to the point that I couldn't function. An old coworker of mine came there that day to assist me. She made calls and found out that there weren't any inspections scheduled that day. That's when I began to realize how much pull the landlord had in the county. A quick google search confirmed this years later. She had given thousands in local political donations. She was also the director on a county board.

The third altercation

I had an alarm system installed in my salon because it was clear I had visitors in the salon (the toilet seat was up as if a man was urinating in it). I got an alert that the alarm was triggered. When I got there, she was in a lilac robe with an intoxicated appearance. She was rambling on and on as I stood in a state of shock with the same old coworker I referenced earlier. Her daughter flew into the salon, literally covering her mothers' mouth while choking her out of the salon simultaneously. They only left because I mentioned her triggering the alarm would result in an officer coming. Once a close source of hers confided in me, I understood what I was dealing with. She had a severe drinking problem (according to the source). That was my "ah-ha" moment.

The fourth altercation

So, by the summer of 2017, the fourth altercation occurred. (HUNNY BAYBAYYYYYY). By the first day of summer, she had her plan. On the hottest day, she cut my air conditioner off. This is significant within a black salon. Hooded dryers are a staple in hair salons that cater to kinky hair. It's essential to prevent direct heat from a blow dryer. So, asking clients to "understand" as they sweat under the hooded dryer is counterproductive and embarrassing. I received permission from the other landlord to purchase a portable air conditioning unit and take it out of the rent. When I did that, not only did she once again forbid me from venting the exhaust out through a hole in the wall, she now was suing me for the rental amount I took out.

Now, under all other circumstances, the landlord looked a complete mess by all standards. Hair all over her head, sweat clothes, baseball hat, etc. When we got to court (YES, this lady actually took us to court), she…looked…FABULOUS. I mean stunning. She looked like she was headed to the opera. Hair done, makeup on point, and a dazzling outfit. The lady looked nothing like the con artist I had grown to despise. I remember her attorney approached me with the assumption I fell behind on my rent. He was attempting to negotiate a payment arrangement. When I told him she cut off the air and why the rent was a few hundred dollars short, his mouth dropped. He actually said he wished he had another client. This was the second (and not the last) time a contractor of hers said disparaging words about her.

Well, I did win that battle because I got the permission to withhold rent from the other landlord in writing. By the time winter of 2017 was approaching, I knew I had to make a decision. My biggest issue was that she would try to sue me for not paying back rent if I abandoned the lease early. I was caught between a rock and a hard place.

Now, I mentioned earlier that I stumbled upon information

that she had a drinking problem. I knew that during a drunken episode, she would run her mouth too much, and that would be my opportunity to escape. I had to weigh out my options. It wasn't worth the fight to stay, in my opinion, because of the following factors:

1. There was a methadone clinic upstairs (the clients were begging my clients for money).

2. We sat adjacent to an infamous transgender prostitute strip. The tricks were approaching my clients and even my dad on an occasion. They would usually party on the corner every weekend – sometimes topless and sometimes in a teddy. Yes, you read all of these things correctly, so read it again a second time.

3. The landlord was an elderly geriatric reality show in the flesh.

4. I could not solicit any new clientele due to these issues.

The opportunity came once I realized she had been asking me to leave 30 days into our lease. So, on November 16, 2017, it was official. We moved out and relocated to a smaller space (saving money) and a better area (no more prostitutes or meth addicts).

What this experience taught me was beneficial to my drive as an entrepreneur. Had I not met that landlord, I would not have learned:

How to deal with the challenges I'd encounter at the new location.

1. How to interact with people you don't like cordially.

2. How to pick a proper location to charge accordingly.

3. How to understand that cotenants are afraid too.

4. How to work with landlords who are bullies.

5. How to balance mental health and business.

So, let me now share what I've learned with you in hopes it will assist you in this journey as an entrepreneur.

Chapter 2

It's a Small World:

Why cordial communication is

necessary

We've always heard that it's a small world. Do you know how many times who I was (Dawn Michelle Williams) was detrimental to a sale? The impression you leave on a client, contractor, or vendor spreads fast. In business, you will always have to ask people from your past for favors. For example, I had a person leave an anonymous review for my snack business that was poor. Since my client list is relatively small, I pretty much know all of my clients. Because it was my first review, it automatically brought my rating down to a 1 star. This looks bad for potential clients. I knew that all I needed was a minimum of 5 clients to give me a 5-star rating. The fact that all I had to do was text a group of people (including in-laws), and I received an almost immediate response spoke volumes.

If you can't call on people from your past for simple favors just off of GP (General Principle), you need to check yourself. Small businesses are almost always dependent upon personal interactions. Years ago, someone who was very nasty to me in a consistent passive-aggressive way (highly manipulative) showed her weakness one day when it came to business. You see, she needed to sell her product and asked me to post a flier at my job. In my mind, there was no question that I could not now push a product for a person I had already told people was nasty towards me. It makes no sense. What I learned after that was that if she had the audacity to ask me for such a favor, she must not have had success asking others.

If you are not a "people person" (meaning you constantly

burn bridges), therapy is the option for you. Learning how to interact with people is a learned skill. If you never practiced this in your youth, you're more than likely stuck in your ways. This is not necessarily due to stupidity or even arrogance, but lack of time practiced. You see, as a mother, I can mold my children in such a way to condition them with manners. For example, I can:

1. Tell my son to speak to clients as they enter my business.

2. Teach my children to own up to mistakes and apologize.

3. Practice problem-solving and anger management drills.

As a grown adult, it then becomes your responsibility. If you lack "home training" as the old school folks say, it has to be taught to you. If you missed it as a child, then as a responsible adult, you can:

1. Conduct verbal polls to your clients.

2. Seek therapy for mental health issues.

3. Hire an etiquette consultant.

4. Surround yourself with a support system that is VERY direct with genuine intentions to point out your faults.

Another important key factor to remember when you are dealing with being cordial with people is networking. Networking isn't always what you see in the media, social media, and Hollywood. Networking is the gas station cashier. Networking is the trash man. Networking is that neighbor across the street. Networking is that client's momma who asked, "who did your hair?" Networking is as simple as listening to a spontaneous husband...like mine, for example.

We are opposites. I am stuck in my ways. Same juice, breakfast, same decor styles, fashion, and the list goes on. Umar is the definition of spontaneous. He always wants to try new foods, go to new places, try new stores, etc. So, I (Mrs. Stuck-in-her-ways) found my mechanic from a networking referral from none other than Umar. Although he tried different mechanics after that, I stayed with the same mechanic he referred to me because of my personality. Referrals are a huge part of business. Even if a client is a mental case (as I have experienced), the fact that I didn't curse them out went a long way. I, in turn, just set boundaries (mandatory deposits, grace periods, etc.). There have been many crazy clients that send referrals because, believe it or not, the referrals were often opposite of the personality that sent them. Now, I am not at all saying Umar is a crazy client. I'm just saying that polar opposites often attract, such as spouses, family members, coworkers, and even friends, who all have the potential to be referrals.

Always remember that the face of networking is not defined. It's the feeling you left the person with after your last interaction. According to Daniel James (source: https://www.furstperson.com/blog/59-of-customers-dont-return-after-a-bad-customer-service-experience), the risk of an unpleasant customer service experience has "59% of customers ceasing business with that company." So, the way you respond to a difficult client can affect your income.

According to Craig Bloem (source: https://www.inc.com/craig-bloem/84-percent-of-people-trust-online-reviews-as-much-.html), "Research shows that 91 percent of people regularly or occasionally read online reviews, and 84 percent trust online reviews as much as a personal recommendation. And they make that decision quickly: 68 percent form an opinion after reading between one and six online reviews." So, as opposed to 20 years ago, the entire world has the capability of destroying your business with bad reviews. Look at how many self-employed businesspeople are caught on camera in horrible lights (having racist outbursts, having angry shouting matches, homophobic and transphobic moments, and so on). For example, in Oregon, Melissa and Aaron Klein closed their bakery in a Portland suburb, Sweet Cakes by Melissa, after being fined $135,000 for refusing to make a wedding cake in 2013 for a lesbian couple.

So, I remember trying to understand this from a business perspective, thinking: "So, you mean to tell me you make enough money to SELECT clients by beliefs, gender, personal opinions or lifestyles?" Do you know how many clients I've serviced not realizing who their significant other was until years later? Why? Because the #1 rule of business is MIND YOUR BUSINESS. Let's use the logic behind this. Now that we're selecting whom we conduct business with based on their personal business, what about your hairdresser? What about your cab driver? How about that trash man? What about the lady who does your nails? How about the Hindu couple who owns the corner store? Ridiculous, right? Let's go further. How about the manufacturer of the egg carton you got? The plumber who installed the toilet at your house upon construction? Did you check to see their religion, gender, or maybe their marital status? How about we see if that lawyer you hired experimented with coke 20 years ago in college? Did you investigate any of these things prior to conducting transactions with them? No? Exactly. Because it's NONE OF YOUR BUSINESS.

Well then, what is my business as an entrepreneur? If the check clears. That's it, and that's all. If your religious convictions interfere with your business, you have two choices:

1. Close your business and open a church, mosque, synagogue or temple.

2. Wait for the government to fine you and close it for you. Then you can open up a church, mosque, synagogue or temple.

Another example is the infamous Uriah's Heating and Cooling owner. He repeated to a man three times "I want to tell you how much of a n#$er you are" after following him to his house. Well, once it went viral, that $500 fine was nothing compared to how his business reputation was destroyed. After all, most of his clientele were black. If the clientele that shared his views could sustain his lifestyle independently, he probably wouldn't have offered a plea to the public for forgiveness. Sure, he can rebrand and make another business. He can even move. But only businesspeople truly know the time it takes to build a reputation, let alone a clientele. It takes years upon years. Even if he changes his government name and business name, most people never forget a face. Why go through all of that for a problem you can proactively solve yourself. My suggestion? You should instead:

1. Seek anger management skills. This can be completed with a therapist.

2. Seek a therapist to help you work out issues, such as racism in this example.

3. Try to use the same language you use at home in public so the two personalities won't cross. For example, if Uriah watches his language when he's kickin' it (hanging out) with his friends, once he gets upset in public, he will be in the practice of displaying appropriate behavior. In other words, the n-word can't "slip out" if you don't use it behind closed doors. Realistically, this is why therapy is needed. To sort out the underlying cause of such volatile behavior.

Business and personal lives are sometimes like oil and vinegar. There is an unsaid separation of the two. So, although my beliefs as a Muslim at times are not a replica of my clients, that has nothing to do with the exchange of money. It's a mutual respect. So much so that when I say, "please excuse me" to perform one of our obligatory prayers, any client of any religion respects the request because they respect me as a person.

When you are self-employed, you are always "on". You have to be ever so aware of the "you" that is presented to the public. So, in actuality, if you are the same "you" all the way around (at home, in your marriage, as a parent, as a customer, as a daughter, as a neighbor), you won't have to put on a performance. This takes years of practice. It will not come overnight. It's a growth process. It's a constant healing process. Entrepreneurship puts all the negative aspects of "you" out there for the public to see, with little room for error in the modern age where information is shared at the click of a literal button.

Chapter 3

Mental Health and Anger Control

Are Key

Being an entrepreneur goes hand in hand with having a clear thought process. A clear thought process goes hand in hand with the ability to make sensible decisions in regard to conducting business.

This is when you have to have an understanding of your team. The people in your circle that are involved with your daily interactions play an integral part within an organization. We are mirrors of each other at times. I believe it is essential that at least one of your key team members is brutally honest. But be careful not to mistake what I'm describing for a person with bad intentions. For example, if I have lipstick on my teeth and my friend pulls me to the side to signal me, it's clear their intent is not to embarrass me. The intent is so I can improve my appearance so as to not give the wrong impression.

Often, it is more effective to hear the cold hard truth than a lie to spare feelings or even a soft cushy sugarcoated version of the truth. In business dealings, time is literally money. I have found that the initial shock of a direct person is easier to handle in the long run. It propels you into action. The words don't leave you stagnant. I grew up in the Baptist Church and remember hearing that life and death is in the power of the tongue. You can literally speak life into someone with truth.

Some time ago, I didn't have custody of my eldest child. The day came when I felt as though I was ready to raise him. Some years had passed, and I had a second child. What was a verbal arrangement (which is why I am insistent on contracts in writing) ended in disaster once I understood that his grandparents changed their minds and no longer wanted me to gain custody. Instead of hearing it verbally (since I was visiting him twice weekly at their house), I instead received a letter from their attorney. When I opened the letter, it was on a day I was supposed to visit my son. I was an emotional wreck. I could not comprehend why this was happening. I remember going on my usual pit stop to my childhood friend's home with my then-toddler prior to visiting my eldest weekly. I cried and cried. She hugged me and gave encouraging words. I called my dad. It was hilarious because he was the king of sugarcoating the truth. He said, "I mean Dawn, are you surprised?" When I cried "YES!!!!", he then said, "How can I put this? It's a dog-eat-dog world. It's every man for himself."

Mind you, I still had to visit the kid within a few hours. When I got there, I was just asking the grandparents what they wanted so I can just give up. I really did not want to fight them at all. I remember the grandfather saying for me to just consult an attorney. I had never felt so stupid in my life. Although there were red flags, we all went out together prior to this day (to the zoo, grocery store, doctor's appointments, etc.). I was so upset this was happening this way.

So, as usual, by 7 pm (they had me on a strict schedule), my dad came to pick me up. He took me all the way from Upper Marlboro to Northwest Washington D.C. I know I was sobbing. It was pathetic. My whole soul spoke through my body language, which was to give up. So, in walks my husband. He asked me what was up, and I remember crying explaining what happened. He cut me off and said, "Life is hard. Get over it. What's the next move?" For some reason, my tears dried up. My friend, who I spoke about earlier, had an attorney. The next morning, Umar got up an extra 30 minutes early to go to the bank and get the retainer fee. He woke me up and left the money as he was leaving to go to work at 6 am!

His hard truth, as well as my dad's, was necessary. It is reality. Crying has too long of a recovery time. So, instead of being upset that I was restricted to a schedule of visiting my son over those years, I used that time to grow a business online. It takes time to research free platforms and make websites. Since I had a toddler and was home a lot, I used that time to concentrate on business. At that time, there was nothing I could do about the custody of my son. So, to waste time dwelling on it would take too long to recover. I lived pretending like it was not a big deal. And you know what? After a while, it wasn't a big deal because I tricked my mind to believe that.

Throughout the custody battle, I didn't understand why this was happening to me, including why so many people were believing the lies told about me. However, it was monumental in my concept of contracts. You see, I don't wake up in the morning on business calls trusting people who haven't proven they're trustworthy. That is what deposits, receipts, and contracts are for. Prior to that custody battle, I was a naive person. Naivety and business don't mix. I automatically think of the worst-case scenario FIRST. For example, if I have to step out of the salon to use the bathroom, and there is a new client there, I grab my purse and take it with me. I don't have time to recover emotionally should I find out later that the client is a thief. If I need something fixed by a landlord, I will generally email first. I do not have the time to invest in recovering from my anger when the landlord says I never asked them to fix it.

I have found that business dealings deal directly with personal dealings. For example, the amount of restraint it takes to not curse a client out who is unreasonable is the same restraint I have to use in personal dealings. There was such a time where I had no restraint and felt entitled to my anger because, in my opinion, the person's ridiculous actions warranted that. Well, that's a bit different when you have children.

I want to use them as an example now. At times, there

have been miscommunications between my children and their teachers. My youngest, for example, was frustrated with a teacher. He was an older man – old enough to be my dad. He had a "Mr. Rogers" disposition about himself. I found that once my son complained about the teacher, it was best to sit down with that teacher. Each and every time we did that, it calmed down tensions. I acted as a liaison to bridge a communication gap. It was actually a lesson in business for my son to not mix emotions when you have a task at hand. This teacher is paid to execute lessons, and we need this child to pass to the next grade. I also had to teach the child that his main objective isn't to like or be friends with the teacher. That is not why he's in school.

For years, I was upset about the way the custody battle went with my eldest son. Anger is a waste of time. Manipulative people or bullies usually only have power through YOUR uncontrolled anger. It wasn't until years later that I realized how the interactions with those people (the grandparents) prepared me. You see, I started viewing people in patterns. I only know what you are capable of based on factual patterns. That's why when my dad asked if I was surprised, it made sense later. I got to think back on the past as I calmed down. I dismissed those red flags I spoke of, assuming she was going through something. In actuality, it was slow, calculated digs over the course of the years, so that once I exploded, all the lies that were being told about me to support their unethical final checkmate could make sense from a third-party perspective.

It took me ten years to understand the mind of a master manipulator, and the "why" I so longed for when I realized I was literally conned. Once I understood "why", I realized what a complete waste of time that was. I mean, ten years? It's a waste of time because you can't convince a master manipulator of foresight. As my dad repeatedly said, you can't reason with insanity. I spent ten years trying to reason with it. Bottom line? They have something they need immediate gratification for. They need it NOW. They'll stop at nothing to get it NOW. So, while

I was crying and simultaneously refraining from exploding, I had the foresight to think that I still wanted to be able to visit this kid throughout the custody trial, or that I still needed to be calm to keep my job (I was the hairstylist at a nursing home). I was thinking of fifteen years from now when the child will ask why I lied and present me with "proof". I was literally avoiding a future confrontation that won't occur for another fifteen years by not exploding on the grandparents.

Time flies, and kids ask questions. This is 2021. Information is searchable. Manipulation is shortsighted because it has an expiration date. The truth adds up now, in ten years or fifty years after your death, and it's consistent. Manipulators think they can have power forever because they can continuously piss you off, but what they don't talk about is the humiliation after everyone calms down. It's embarrassing for them. The anger I felt diminished simply because it's a waste of time. Truth comes out eventually. When I won custody of my son, I remember my dad saying "See, I told you the truth would come out."

During the trial, I had to sit in a completely frozen state as I watched blood relatives testify against me with lies and speculation. One relative testified against me with knowledge of only being around me personally less than five times yearly. They didn't know me personally at all. Only through the eyes of false speculative whisper campaigns did they have an alleged glimpse of my reality. My attorney coached me to sit still and not make facial expressions. I remember it was Ramadan (the fasting time for Muslims). There is something about not eating and anger control. It helped me greatly. My husband often jokes with me about those times. He said only a true psychopath could sit perfectly still as that chaos was happening.

Anger control and problem-solving go hand in hand. I'll end this chapter with a story about my youngest child. We are in a district with virtual learning for the pandemic. The youngest was frustrated because the assignments he did complete did not reflect the grades in the online system. I asked him to look at this from another perspective. It seems as if children respond better to giving different problem-solving techniques. I gave him this scenario:

I had two clients who had ten appointments throughout the year, and one ALWAYS showed up. The other showed up only seven times out of the ten. The times she didn't show up, she didn't call to tell me she wasn't coming. After the third no show, do you think I would:

1. *Take her seriously?*

2. *Put her appointments ahead of the faithful clients?*

3. *Give her any more appointments?*

4. *Pick up the phone in haste when she calls for appointments?*

He sat still, and I saw the wheels turning. I then explained that once he missed one assignment, he was automatically categorized in the "not to be taken seriously" pile. I also explained that the teacher in question was not very internet savvy, meaning it may take her longer to input grades or make lesson plans than the other teachers. So, instead of demanding for the teachers to input grades faster, wouldn't it make more sense to keep those assignments at top priority? So, the teacher has in her mind, "Oh, I already know he is going to turn this in, so I don't have to worry about him." Business has a lot to do with problem-solving. Manipulation is a predictable pattern. Intelligence uses innovations to solve patterns. It's foresight.

Chapter 4
Taking Advice
Constructive criticism

Lolita's story

I'm going to kick this chapter off with my client Lolita (Listwithlolita.com). The first location for my salon was on Eastern Avenue. This is a street that divides Northeast D.C. and Maryland. It's not the prettiest of areas, but I didn't care – I was paying $1200 a month, and it was my spot. It didn't take long before the prostitutes came out on the strip. Transgender prostitutes. I had passed the point of embarrassment once my 7 am FAITHFUL client Lolita got out of her car. We walked up to the building. I saw the trick, but I pretended not to see her. Lolita said, "Is that a prostitute?!!" We both fell out laughing. I was mortified, but it needed to be said. I mean, why was I okay with the salon being on a literal prostitute strip?

Another time, I remember I was going through some stuff with that psychopath of a landlord (mentioned in chapter 1). That 750 square foot salon got really big and tedious to keep clean. That was no excuse, though. Lolita didn't hesitate to let me know either. We walked in the salon together. She took one look at my front desk and told me I should clean it off because it was a mess. The importance of receiving criticism is the fact that some people say what others will not. Often, clients will go to another salon without saying a word. You just have to realize it once they stop coming back.

Over the years, I learned to take her direct demeanor as essential constructive criticism. She wanted to see her stylist grow. How do I know? She ALWAYS tells people about me. She has sent countless referrals. Constructive criticism is founded on intent.

Taking advice is key to how you will grow as an entrepreneur. I have found the following effective strategies:

1. Only take advice from someone who has successfully advised someone in the same manner.

2. Only take advice if the person giving advice is where you want to be or has genuine intentions.

I remember in my early years as a hairstylist when someone close to me was balding. She went to a doctor that had a product line that would help people to reverse thinning hair. The most ridiculous part of this was the fact that the owner of the company had his picture on the products. HE WAS BALDING!! Not a shaved bald head, but a clearly receding hairline. That made absolutely no sense. How can he tell her how to grow her hair when he couldn't and didn't help himself? This was a straight-up con artist.

Secondly, a mechanic we had (prior to the one my husband found previously) held us up one day preaching about marriage advice. He was going on and on, and I sat there and listened with Umar. We then found out he was speaking as a divorced man. What advice can you tell me about staying in a marriage to last the test of time when you're divorced? Sure, he can tell us what mistakes he made, but the formula for the marriage to last? He isn't capable of offering first-hand advice.

Another example is a professor I had in college. He used to teach what he did in his restaurant. I remember one example of him taking water bottles, filling them up with tap water, and charging for it. It wasn't until I was midway through the course when he said he had failed businesses. I was around 20 years old, thinking, "How can he tell me about how to have a thriving business when his is closed?"

These three examples are so indicative of the many people I've encountered over the years. After a while, I started being selective on whose advice I would consider. This is essential for business. Not using these strategies has cost me money. When you plan out a business venture, it is best to consult with someone who is where you want to be. This is not all-inclusive. For example, the mechanic isn't where I want to be in regard to relationships, but I'd take advice for business from him. The professor may not be sought after for business advice, but perhaps I can consult with him for connections or how to market my book to universities. Business isn't necessarily about declaring someone useless, as networking can highlight great qualities in everyone.

I was recently talking to my eldest son, who is 14. He was trying to reason with me about how now he is mature enough to meet deadlines I need. He is excellent at web design and things of that nature. But if I say I need a commercial by Tuesday, 9 times out of 10, that won't happen. I explained to him that it isn't something to feel bad about. Instead, I highlighted his strengths. I explained that he was my #1 consultant. I know for certain he will sit and teach me how to design things, utilize websites, and understand HTML codes, but his brother is the key person for deadlines. I don't know what type of alarm my youngest baby has in his brain. He never lets me miss a deadline if he is involved. He is like a miniature alarm. That is his gift, and technical support is my eldest son's gift.

Not taking advice from the right people can also stop your income. It was Einstein who said that insanity is doing the same thing over and over expecting a different result. I know it took four years for me to finally ask the declutter king (Umar) what needed to be done for my salon space to look nice. I had to swallow my pride and let him be brutally honest about what needed to change. Clients sometimes will not want to hurt your feelings. He ripped me to shreds, criticizing the excessive signs everywhere, the chips tacked on the wall, excessive products, the trash can places being wrong, and more. Then, after I finished, I had the eldest son come in and continue to rip me to shreds. He is the declutter prince. His assessment was so crazy I recorded it. The result was immediate. Clients loved it. The important thing is that since they enjoyed their experience, they are more likely to refer others.

Sometimes, people will not offer you advice because you are not approachable. As I said, it took me four years to ask for my husband's advice. So, although he may not have experience in business, he had experience in decluttering and noticing small details everywhere we go. I had a client soon after that suggested client appreciation bags. She specifically said I needed to get bags that look like presents. She added that she was hesitant to mention it before because she didn't want to offend me. I told her that I appreciated the advice and quickly did a campaign. The clients loved it. I had numerous clients say they never had a hairstylist give them customer appreciation bags. So, again, although this client didn't have a business of her own, her advice was valuable because she offered the perspective of a client, which I did not have.

The goal should not be mediocrity. It should be to give your client an experience that leaves them smiling afterward. After all, it is terrifying at times being an entrepreneur. If there is one thing you should have learned during the pandemic of 2020, it's that you are on your own. If you are blessed enough to still have clients afterward, they should be shown appreciation. There is this YouTuber I have been following on Instagram for some time. You know how you can't comprehend what someone is saying until a mitigating circumstance is presented? This influencer always spoke about selling retail products after your client's service. I watched it, thinking I couldn't do it. It's amazing how the passing of my dad rearranged my thinking.

I then started to look at myself and ask "Why can't I do that?" Why can't I charge new clients $100 for a relaxer? I then asked Umar for the advice about the salon. It was a ripple effect, like a healing of the mind. I was mourning, grieving, and healing, all in the same breath. I did not have time to recover from the anger from the death of my daddy. I was now a mommy. I did not have the option of falling apart. I had two kids, a husband, a dog, a cat, and businesses that needed to get off the ground. Mediocrity was not an option.

I then started thinking about business pricing. Make-up artists charge $100 for a face that will be gone by the morning. We went to the Baltimore Aquarium and paid $150 to see something we can't take home. If we go to a movie theatre, it would cost us $100 for tickets, parking, and popcorn. Even going to Red Lobster was $80-$100. So why can't I get my $100 for a relaxer?

The experience was not a $100 experience. So, I started making it a $100 experience by:

- Introducing online booking.

- Offering complimentary snacks (sparkling juice, mints, crackers, cookies, coffee).

- Upgrading internet content.

- Redesigning the retail shelving on the walls.

- Getting an opt-in text line

- Purchasing more professional attire.

- Putting a mini TV up with digital signs to replace paper signs.

- Putting in a mini phone charging station.

Think about it. I would have never changed my thinking if I had not taken advice from others.

A last bit of advice I want to personally give is that of my client. She listened to my grievance about my ongoing custody issue. I remember her saying that no one wants to hear your problems, or something to that degree. Now, some clients do want to hear and even offer help. I've received great advice from those that do. But to not scare new clients off. It's best not to go too deep into your drama for new clients (meaning less than two years as a client). It takes years for people to get to know you. YEARS. Don't hit them with your personal affairs all at once. You will quickly find that there are only a handful of clients who truly want to advise you or that can even handle knowing your faults without using them against you. Many just want to talk about the weather or politics.

Chapter 5

Clients and Contractors Who Are Bullies

Clients who are bullies are easy to handle. You have two choices:

1. You can fire them.

2. You have the power to create a rule for your own peace of mind.

This is why deposits are required for hotel bookings, car rentals, or even make-up artist services. Gone are the days of expecting clients to be honest. It's amazing how people remember an appointment or reservation once they have paid a deposit first. That's because they value the money before they value your time. You, as the owner, have the obligation of putting value over your own time. Your phone should be on "do not disturb" after a certain time. Clients should not have 24-hour access to your life. Instead, you can have automated means to handle clients, such as:

1. An online booking system with confirmations sent.

2. Auto-replies for emails and text messages.

3. Electronic payment platforms (PayPal, Cash App, or Zelle, for example).

Bullying can either make or break you. If you do not know how to deal with bullies, this career path will chew you up and spit you out. I'll begin with a rule of thumb. Clients or contractors who are bullies treat everyone with the same personality type the exact same way. Bullying is a problem-solving tactic. It took me years to understand this. People who are not bullies usually use innovative methods to effectively solve problems. Bullies use tactics that are proactive in regard to concealing their inability to solve problems with smokescreens (also known as stalling tactics). The number one tactic is to press your buttons. This is because they have already prepared how they will react to your volatile reaction. What they are not prepared for is if you do not have a volatile reaction and are stern as well while setting serious boundaries.

I'll start with a story of a salon I worked at as an independent contractor. This was back in 2009. I worked on Old Central Avenue in Capitol Heights, Maryland. I was starting over. At that time, I didn't have custody of my eldest. I was a newlywed, and we just had our son, who was about 6 months old. The owner at the time had two salon locations (both have since closed). When I went to apply for a booth, it was at the location in D.C. This was on H Street NE, right at the beginning of the regentrification. He was at a prime location with plenty of walk-ins. When I got there, that shop was jumping. Guys were literally jumping out of the front door from lively excitement. I was so excited to be back in an atmosphere like that one. I hadn't worked at a salon in over a year.

I remember I had pictures of free hairstyles I had done to prove to the owner that I could do hair even though I didn't have any clientele. He loved the pictures. Since I was licensed, I was hired on the spot and began working at the location soon after. I remember my dad driving me past the salon to see it. It looked pretty basic, and the bars on the windows didn't help the appearance.

The salon had no walk-in traffic – there was absolutely no one coming in the salon. I remember after brainstorming with my husband, we decided to make a sign made of particle board. It was his idea to paint it yellow with black letters. This was because we saw a similar sign near Rhode Island Avenue NE, D.C. on one car ride home that caught his attention. So, there I was in the middle of a heatwave painting a sign outside of this salon. The manager and one other employee were laughing at me. Even the clients (who only went to the manager) were joining in.

Finally, I finished and set it outside on the sidewalk. It said "1(866)999-4246 FREE HAIRSTYLES". All of a sudden, traffic started rolling in. The manager was upset – it was not supposed to work in her eyes. When they came in, I would hand them a flier, tell them that the free hairstyles would be raffled away at a cookout two months later, then wait. They almost always ask how much a hairstyle would cost then and there. Once I said $30, it was on. They sat right in the chair.

So, as we always know, all bullies have their "showdown" day. It arrived when 5-6 people came in less than two hours inquiring about my sign. At that point, the manager proceeded to walk over and direct a client to my coworker (who didn't have clients). Of course, my issue was the fact that if the client came in solely because of seeing my sign, then it's my client. She disagreed. So soon after, a meeting was called to discuss me. There was no compromise. No one would help me lug that sign out or put it back. No one would reimburse me for the sign. I couldn't get a commission off of the income generated by my sign. I had to surrender, allowing everyone in the shop to benefit off of my sign as long as I was on commission. I gave in and never took the sign out again. The salon went back to being dead. No clients. I left soon after.

Later on, the thing I learned was that I wasn't an employee. In the state of MD, I am only considered an employee if the owner controls the financial part of the transaction. If the contractor takes their own payments, they are a contractor. They were putting stipulations on me that they weren't entitled to based on my ignorance of the law. I have found that more often than not, business contractors bully people into horrible positions solely due to ignorance of the law. It's even more difficult when an attorney is needed. You will more than likely not be able to find a pro bono business attorney. You have to research things, and you have to know how to utilize your research. For example, it's one thing to know the laws of your state regarding eviction. It's an entirely different game knowing how to utilize it.

This brings me to another situation I had with a commercial landlord. The entrance to the building had a door that was faulty. When I had first arrived, I didn't pay close attention. Besides, I was so excited to be leasing at the location. From all outward appearances, it had an elegant first impression. I remember the property manager making, quite honestly, some really good excuses for what we were looking at. She said something to the effect of "The key fob sometimes acts up." Six months later, I would come to understand what exactly was happening. In actuality, the door had turned on us. The door was so faulty that my co-tenants and I would be standing outside not able to gain entry to the building. Once it got to the point where at 6 am I couldn't get in, I reached out to the district property manager. After all, the on-site manager was just complaining like us.

After months of written correspondence, it was clear that:

1. The managers didn't care.

2. The owner didn't care.

When you are the owner or a contractor, and your landlord doesn't care, usually the next step is to move. We are a society of runners. For years, I found myself running from salon to salon, vowing to get my own salon to escape the con games. It was astounding to find that once I reached the goal I longed for, it didn't solve that problem. Why? Because landlords and property owners used the same type of bullying tactics that my prior supervisors used. It's easier to trick you into thinking there is no problem than to actually solve the problem. As I said before, bullying is a problem-solving tactic. It is a never-ending stalling tactic because all you have to do is keep getting new clients (or tenants) until word spreads about your poor business practices. That takes years, if not decades, depending on how effective the managers are at tricking people.

Getting back to the story, as my requests proceeded to get ignored, the property took a drastic turn for the worse. Since the door was faulty, homeless people in the areas started living in the facility. I am not kidding. By 8 pm on Saturdays, they started piling in and roaming the building. Soon after, the cleaning lady stopped coming. It went from a few times weekly to none. I'd be walking into the building stepping over piles of trash. I started arriving early to clean the building prior to my client's arrival. As if this weren't enough, we started to not have any soap in the bathrooms. I started handing my clients toilet paper and soap when they said they had to use the restroom as if we were in a homeless shelter.

At that point, I had enough – it was time for a showdown. Interestingly enough, my co-tenants weren't as vocal as I was. You see, in business, emails and letters are essential. Why? Because a paper trail is powerful when it comes to legal matters. I started contacting government agencies. This is because all businesses in the United States must go through some form of licensing in order to legitimately collect income. In actuality, the United States is set up like a business model. It just lies on the side of business that concentrates on liability protection. They don't want citizens suing them for not intervening in certain matters.

You see, the game changed once I lost the first client due to the incompetence of the owner of the business. That one client (who was paying market rate for services) complained each and every time she used the bathroom. She kept saying that the bathroom was filthy. I brushed it off as not my problem since I didn't want to ruffle any feathers at this commercial location. It occurred to me that if I lose my entire clientele, this man would still want full rent. So, why would I allow him to strip me of my power (clientele, aka the ability to move to another location)? Thus, my quest for a resolution started.

I also want to mention their eviction tactics. These people contracted workers who would come in and illegally disconnect electricity from the circuit breaker. They would even open up the high voltage unit to disconnect electricity and force late tenants to pay on time or to put out whoever they needed gone. My neighbors had to call the police after they tried to change the locks to her suite while she was simultaneously servicing a client.

I contacted the governor, county executive, landlord, the owners, the municipality, the fire marshal, the state board of licensing, and even my co-tenants. I was causing so much disruption that they demanded I leave. I was so scared. I remember asking long term tenants what happened to the previous tenants who complained. They told me that they were locked out and illegally evicted. So, in other words, the owners, as well as his partners and staff, were bullies. They scared their tenants into quiet submission until they decided to move or were put out. I remember the day I was supposed to move, I sat in the salon eating popcorn and watching Netflix. This is because a few days prior, I sent a certified letter to the owner. Through research, I found out that:

1. It is illegal for a landlord to evict you for asking to repair things.

2. They were not licensed properly anyway.

3. They were in violation of fire codes.

I also found out that he was entangled in a lawsuit with multimillion-dollar investors. He was ripping off investors as well! To add insult to injury, this was a black man. Every time I told this story to ask for help, everyone (and I mean everyone) assumed he was a white man. It's so naive that we as African Americans think that other black folk in our community have some sort of morality just because they're millionaires. When I say we, I mean me. I had this ridiculous notion that somehow money made people have some level of common sense or foresight.

It is not enough to shout or even talk to the owner about the legal protection I had come across. It is REQUIRED by the school of business and common sense to send what you found in writing (certified or email). This is for one reason. Every businessperson knows courts take emails seriously. Do not send important things that need to be discussed via text message. It must be an email. This alleged businessman knew I was lining him up for a lawsuit, and I never had to say it one time for him to arrive at that conclusion. The paper trail said it for me.

They did not have the legal grounds to put me out. The funny thing is, they only sent an intent letter. These people actually put their illegal eviction practices in the initial contract that all tenants sign. Another thing I learned was that you cannot expect a court of law to enforce an illegal contract. So, in actuality, this landlord operated on the premise of scare tactics. If he threw in your face what you signed, you would cower over out of fear. This is an effective tactic. The problem is, once you find the lunatic in the group (me), you will have a hard time getting rid of them. In fact, they were very upset after I didn't move. They tried a few more annoying tactics, but I didn't care. The door got fixed because I complained relentlessly, the manager was put out, we had soap in the bathroom again, and we now had a cleaning lady who showed up regularly.

I didn't even care that my cotenants had distanced themselves from me due to fear of retaliation from the owner. One day, it hit them in the face. Five tenants simultaneously left within 30 days. We're talking thousands of dollars on a monthly basis gone! I was chuckling inside. I already knew they were leaving because they secretly told me. Afterward, the owner started falling back into the old habits. The cleaning lady started disappearing again. I made a comment, and it was met with swift opposition. Afterward, I sent an email saying that silence doesn't always equal loyalty. I explained how it was ridiculous that they are confused when my complaints force them to improve, therefore retaining long-term tenants. I asked if they think the next five tenants will warn them? Truth be told, I refused to move anyway. The key reason why is because I polled my clients. The majority of them liked the location. So, moving would have been an emotional move due to my own pride. The key to business is pleasing clients. They keep your business going.

After that conversation, the landlord called me. We came to a mutual understanding. I bombed her out really bad, and she apologized. It was a monumental moment for me. I truly understood how to take emotion out of decisions and communicate with them to get problems solved effectively.

Chapter 6
Family, Mental Health, and Licensing

I touched on access in an earlier chapter. Clients should have restricted access to you. Remember, clients are not your supervisor. It is the same once it is in reverse – you are not their supervisor either. It's a mutual contract between two parties. If your family day is Sunday, then your cell phone should be on silent on Sunday. If you die tomorrow, your client will find another contractor to fulfill the services you provide. Family is first, especially if you have children. Thirty years from now, you will not remember much about all the clients you've served. You don't want your children to hold resentment for the lack of time you had available for them due to servicing clients. Those eighteen years go by quickly. Being an entrepreneur means you can manipulate your schedule. If you can't, it's no one's fault but your own. If you are your own boss, then there is no one to blame but you for such things.

The thought processes of business owners are a bit unconventional. It's not for the faint of heart. Everyone is not meant to be self-employed. It requires you to be an efficient problem solver. Manipulation doesn't go far in business. This is because complaints are a keystroke away.

Your mental health goes hand in hand with being a business owner. It's not like going to work. You are the owner, so you have to be there to open. What's scary about that is that you experience the same problems everyone else does. You just have to be on display and perform more efficiently than an employee. You have to have the ability to be on the phone one minute in an argument, then the next minute floating into your business as if nothing happened. You have to be able to turn it off at the drop of a dime. The key is to schedule a time to think about the problem so that it won't affect your performance. For example, there are moments when my children may need intervention like assistance with schoolwork. It's best to wait until after work to begin brainstorming about ways to solve the problem.

The separation of business and your personal life reminds me of an incident with the first salon location I had. I was naive in giving the landlord my home telephone number. I made the mistake of thinking we were friends. I gave her my home number for cases of emergency (fire, break-in, etc.). Boy, was I surprised when the owner called me to complain that I was putting "too much garbage" in the garbage cans. I was appalled that she didn't have the decency to hold off interrupting my home life to appease her. Clients will attempt to do this as well.

I remember one day I was engaged in a conversation with my son. A client began to repeatedly call my cell phone. I refused to answer it. It was my day off, and I was talking with my son. I also was not going to explain this to my client. My son then asked me to answer the call. I did answer it after he requested for me to answer the phone. Long story short, she was demanding an appointment at a specific time. I decided to accommodate her. Of course, she didn't show up to the appointment. This was a valuable lesson. People will not hold your time at priority. Only you hold the sense of urgency over your time.

It's important to always perform at a 9 out of 10 on most days when it comes to your clients. This is because if and when a family emergency does arise, your clients will understand. If you are consistently underperforming, then your margin for error is small. Everyone makes mistakes. You must understand, a business owner's reaction to mistakes can make or break your business. It's also essential for you to understand that there are only certain clients who are privy to your personal matters.

This can also decrease clientele. Often, clients come to business locations to escape their own drama in exchange for a relaxed environment.

Licensing goes hand in hand with family priorities. First, we must understand the reason why licensing is mandatory. Licensing protects you from liability. I'm reminded of an incident that occurred while I was employed at a nursing home I contracted out of. At the time, I was going upstairs to service clients who were not physically able to come downstairs to the salon. There was a patient who called down to the salon for me to cut his hair. I remember there was a buzz going around involving this patient. It was strange. One of the nurses called down. At the time, she was a client of mine. She told me that if I serviced this client, I needed to throw away my clippers afterward. I was taken aback by this suggestion and asked why would I throw my clippers away for a service that is $15. She refused to tell me. It was due to HIPPA. The Health Insurance Portability and Accountability Act of 1996 (HIPAA) is a federal law that requires the creation of national standards to protect sensitive patient health information from being disclosed without the patient's consent or knowledge.

I couldn't figure out what was going on until a coworker pulled me to the side. She told me he was on contact isolation due to having full-blown AIDS. She also said that even if I wanted to cut his hair, the scalp was full of lesions, pus, and blood. It would have been nearly impossible. Do you know that even with the knowledge of what I just shared with you, another senior staff member tried to force me to come upstairs to cut this man's hair? We actually argued in the hallway. I was a contractor through a company. I threatened to walk off the job and resign due to this. After that, I realized that the handbook for the company I worked for instructed us to NOT go into patients' rooms for services. That was my first line of protection. I didn't come to understand the second line of protection until some years later.

At the same facility, there was a sweet elderly lady. She fell at home and had a bruise on her head that swelled into a puss bubble. A staff member again tried to force me to service this client. I refused due to common sense. I will not scrub a client's scalp with a puss bubble because it may erupt and become a hazardous situation. I then googled Maryland laws regarding cosmetology. It stated that if we as cosmetologists service clients with hazardous conditions in their head (blood, puss, legions, etc.), we could, in fact, lose our licenses. That was when I realized that it served as liability protection. I believe most Americans do not understand the concept of laws within the United States. The underlying reason for laws is liability protection and not necessarily preventative measures as we assume.

Licensing also ensures that other people who want to stop your hustle simply cannot. In this day and age, everyone in business has some form of social media. Unless you have a serious clientele, it is almost impossible to operate off the grid. Going back to liability protection, states, municipalities, and federal agencies have the potential to be liable for accidents within a business structure. Anyone can sue for anything. If a case is argued right by the right attorney at the right time, government agencies will have to pay out for damages. So, if a state is aware that a doctor is operating without a license, they may not say anything. The moment when they are forced to intervene is once a paper trail has commenced.

Licensing and jealousy go hand in hand. When a person is jealous of you or your business, they will try to stop you from making money at all costs. This includes calling to report you conducting business without a license. You need permission at the state, local, and federal level to operate a business in the United States of America. When you decide to go into business, you must take on this responsibility. Sometimes, it seems as if this is too much to handle. That's where your support system comes into play. It took me years to understand this, which is why I formulated the system within "The Research Departments™".

It assists people by helping the maneuver through everyday situations, such as:

1. Family problems (elderly care, marriage, children, and extended family).

2. Landlord-tenant issues.

3. Workplace bullying.

4. Creating digital content for your business.

Another story of licensing that comes to mind is a nursing home salon I worked out of as a contractor. A new manager came aboard the company. To be honest, there was a high turnover. This is because literally no one in the beauty industry aspired to be a hairstylist in a nursing home (except Dawn Williams). After being in the hair industry for over a decade, I came to realize I hated all the drama involved with it. I needed to be able to do hair, which is all I really wanted to do since I was a child. I also wanted to do so without all the ridiculous antics. So, after the birth of my second child, I decided to return to doing hair in a nursing home. I tried it at 18, then was turned off because it wasn't my definition of glamor.

This time was different. I knew I could doll up these senior citizens, build networking simultaneously, and have peace of mind because I was a unicorn. I was licensed, wanted to actually be there, was respectful to the patients, minded my business, and could actually do hair. The added plus was the fact that I could do "Ethnic hair" (as the company described). Hair that grows out of the scalp of brown people is diverse and quite amazing. It is not a cookie-cutter approach to cosmetology like that of the straight-haired mannequin we were practicing on in cosmetology school in 1999. It is like putting a puzzle together on someone's head. Sometimes, they themselves don't know how to begin to fix their own proverbial puzzle. In a nursing home, there was usually one GNA (geriatric nursing assistant) to 10-15 patients.

They barely had time to comb a white patient's hair, let alone through kinky curly tresses of the brown patients. It was a match made in heaven.

Plus, I had a toddler. I couldn't (and honestly didn't want to) work long hours because I needed to spend time with the baby. I also needed a strict schedule because my eldest was in the primary custody of his paternal grandparents. So, every Wednesday and Sunday, I wanted to be at their house to visit my son. I did that for years. Those visitations dictated my work schedule for years. No exceptions.

Anyhow, this manager came on the scene and immediately began to micromanage. She wanted detailed reports and other things that weren't necessary. I want to put this in complete perspective for you. My paychecks were at the most $300 for a two-week period. This chick was tripping. I had to hustle hard for that $300. I am not exaggerating when I say, in order to pull that $300, I was servicing a minimum of 10-15 patients for the day. That was 2-3 times weekly. Sometimes, I'd have five patients in the salon at one time and have to get them out within two hours. It sounds ridiculous, right? But you would have to be there to see how fast I was turning those heads. Quick reference: fifteen years prior, I worked for a lady who monopolized the shampoo assistants, therefore forcing us to fend for ourselves. Well, a decade later, that came in handy. I know how to rotate clients by myself without breaking a sweat.

So, back to the crazy manager. I started digging, and I found out that the salon was not licensed! This was so ironic. This was a valuable lesson learned. People who come out swinging off the bat are usually hiding something. Most of the time, it's incompetence. So, let me tell you. When this coke addict of a manager kept coming for me, I hit them with the license thing. How I'm "In fear of losing my license" working at an unlicensed establishment. You see, any businessperson who keeps themselves busy (such as myself) does not have time to go out of their way to torture people. If I do go about torturing with passive-aggressive tactics, it's solely for retaliation and to buy myself some peace. You see, psychopaths like that manager not only find enjoyment with torturing people, it also buys time. For what, you say? From the moment in time in which you think they're competent until the moment in time where all the incompetence is revealed. It's what my husband likes to call "selling em' def" or, in other words, bluffing.

This heffa was a con artist. The key to silencing a con artist is to keep them busy. They're idiots. They don't have foresight, they only see immediate gratification. So, the quieter you are, the less likely they are to see your attack coming. I kept her busy by forcing her to now have to get the salon licensed. A problem the company hadn't had since the conception of the business. Do you think when a hairstylist goes into a salon, they're looking to see if the business is licensed? Absolutely not! It is assumed that you have a license because you had the audacity to advertise on a public platform.

So now the psycho was busy. She was pissed. Then, she still started to come for me. What this chick did next was out of this world. She picked a day I was working during prime time to come in to clean the salon. Remember, it had to get ready for inspection because of her. Since there was no corporate location nearby, their managers just traveled by car from salon to salon. They dominated the salon nursing homes at the time. In the middle of cleaning, she started intentionally throwing away my personal supplies. In the process, she tossed my client's oil.

This oil belonged to my client, who was a flight attendant. This client was way more efficient than me. She taught me the power of a paper trail way before that manager galloped into town. That oil came from Dubai. The client and I met through networking because her dad was a resident at the facility. She was pissed. She kept asking, and I brushed her off until it hit me. Why should she not be reimbursed? So, as I asked for reimbursement, the manager put up a fight. She then said she would mail the cash in an envelope. I told her that was ridiculous. She came up there on a day I wasn't there to give the cash in a sealed envelope to a coworker I didn't trust. I made sure I opened the envelope while a worker recorded the event with my phone. My, my, my, what a surprise it was that the heffa shorted me. Yeah, it was only $2 short, but I asked for a money order for a certain amount. You see, the power dynamic shifted. I could either sit on this footage or send it to the corporate office. She was so arrogant she just knew I'd call her and ask, "Did you know you shorted me!?!?" She'd play innocent then record me or something, saying I'm a crazy Muslim terrorist.

I wish I could have been a fly on the wall when she saw that email I sent! I attached the video while simultaneously demanding a money order. I got the money order, and the lady was removed from the position. The salon was licensed, so now all was good, and I could continue servicing the elderly clients in peace.

Chapter 7

Utilizing Your Resources

Many people do not understand the power of being kind. Your first resource is your smile. Your clientele relies greatly on how they feel once they enter, during their stay, and as they exit the transaction. That wonderful experience and a kind disposition to accompany it is enough to send their aunt, mom, brother, or co-worker your way. Ask yourself this: if you went to visit someone in an area you didn't know well, you needed to buy some gas, and a close friend was next to you, wouldn't you ask where the nearest gas station is? Many people ask a friend prior to searching for it online. I would rather trust the word of a close friend than that of a stranger or Google.

Now, let's dig a bit deeper. When you are in business, it is not a secret society. Everyone should know what you do, and I mean everyone. Your neighbors, mailman, grocer, mechanic, and teachers at your child's school should know to start with. Do you know how many times I've mentioned in a conversation that I'm a hairstylist or mentioned my clients? Most of the time, they ask for more information after such a statement. I would say about 50% of the time, I've actually convinced someone to come to be serviced. Think about how much of a smaller success rate I would have had if I was mean to those people the first time we met. The first impression means a great deal. People always remember how you made them feel the first time you met.

It is essential to embrace the clients who always send you referrals. These people speak highly of you. These clients should always receive rewards, or at the very least continuous thank-you's. I had a client who I serviced for years. I remember she decided she would become a jewelry consultant. She came in and asked if she could set up a jewelry display in my salon. I agreed. When she asked how much I wanted to be compensated, I told her nothing. I had many people tell me that was a bad decision. I had a strong feeling I shouldn't charge her. It took me months to realize that it was indeed the right decision. Here are reasons why:

1. She came once a month for services ($50).

2. She started bringing her grandson after a while ($30-$70).

3. She came to my housewarming and grand opening (moral support and gift).

4. She assisted me in the home buying process (she was studying to be a realtor).

5. She always refers her loved ones to me.

6. She sent me my electrician.

7. She always supports my other ventures (with payment or referrals).

A few jewelry sales commissions couldn't compare to the value of having her as a client. I would be a complete fool to charge her. The business connection is too deep to sever ties or risk severing ties over a few dollars. I was happy to have the jewelry in my salon. I even upgraded the board to a classy one. Too often, we think the concept of business is charging everyone. Everyone needs a team at some point to excel to a different level in their business.

For example, in order for my business to grow, I needed babysitting often. For a certain number of years, my eldest was being raised by his paternal grandparents. I didn't have him with me as a result. At the time, I couldn't do anything about it since I was restricted to a specific schedule implemented by the grandmother. I was upset for a while until I realized Allah was giving me this time for a reason. I knew then that once I became busy with a future business (that didn't exist yet), I wouldn't have time to do certain things. Much of that time at home with the new baby was spent setting up online resources. I located many of the free services that I use today during that time. I became absorbed in my business. So, although it was a resource I couldn't control, it was a resource.

Everyone around me had a resource to donate, whether it was intentional or unintentional. My dad, in-laws, and co-workers all played an integral part in the support system that restarted my career. Going back to resources, these same people who were there as I had to rebuild my character played a part in me regaining custody of my son. Because I was just being Dawn, it wasn't an act. So, upon meeting them, I was nice just for the sake of being nice. I wasn't thinking that I may need these people later on. I just was being nice because that is who I am. When you go to court and need character witnesses, it isn't easy, especially if you've burned many bridges. That was when I came to realize how many people loved me versus how many didn't.

There were countless people who didn't hesitate to write letters on my behalf. I was shocked that the ones who volunteered to testify were not who I expected. I had a coworker who asked if I needed them to come. I was too scared to ask anyone, although it was necessary for character references. The biggest character reference was my husband's uncle. He was elderly. Everyone knows that elderly folk won't usually vouch for a liar. That man watched me from the moment we met. Elderly folks study people and feel energy from people. So, while this generation considers that an empath, elderly people have been doing that for years. He studied me as I took care of my youngest son. He was there for the night baths and morning feedings. He was there watching me make doctor's appointments and juggle work. So, when I asked him if my son could live at his house with us, he didn't hesitate to say yes. The evidence was clear once the judge considered the fact that:

1. I had an elderly person testifying on my behalf.

2. I had been married for some time.

3. I had a new baby that was thriving in preschool.

It was clear that although the other side launched a smear campaign against me, I had met my burden of proof. Seven years later, every person who was at that hearing said yes when I asked them to support this very book you are reading. That is the true definition of networking and resources.

You see, business isn't always about money. Business is mixed in with friendship, family, acquaintances, and friends. Business is about the true definition of loyalty. There are countless people that have known me from when I was a child that wouldn't hesitate to vouch for me.

Resources aren't just utilized with people who like you. There are many people in business who I personally do not like for legitimate reasons. Those reasons get set to the side when it's time to conduct business. Emotions (mainly anger) do not gel well with business. There are so many people who have done horrible things to me, and later on, came to help me. The key is that you have to maintain boundaries. So, although I may forgive those people, that doesn't mean I trust them for certain things. Let me give an example. Just because I trust my client to pay doesn't mean I trust them to watch my children. It also doesn't mean I trust them with my house keys. Trust has to be selective in business.

One way I was not utilizing my resources was by consistently turning money down. I had been working in a nursing home for years as a stylist. I remember praying for another way to make extra income. At the same time, residents' family members always asked if I did house calls. I always said no because I felt that it was too much effort. One day, a patient caregiver asked me, and I felt I should say yes. After servicing this lady, I managed to secure a standing appointment every two weeks. That is when it occurred to me that I needed to get a second car (which I still have) so I could be reliable. I came up with a system to pack the supplies in my car, and before I knew it, I was bringing in an extra few hundred dollars monthly.

There came a day with this client when an altercation took place. That man, the caregivers, and the accountant were at war. Once it came to the police being called, I politely fired that client because I didn't want to expose myself to all that drama. I had kids, for goodness sake. The interesting part was that I am still in contact with those caregivers until this very day. I still get client referrals from these caregivers. If I was the type to consistently burn bridges, I wouldn't receive enough referrals to stay in business.

One aspect of business is the fact that people are fickle. Many people change their minds as quickly as the wind blows. Keep your mind focused on appreciating the ones who value you. Pamper your clients. Buy them customer appreciation gifts. Once you get to the point of being unavailable due to an influx of clients and those who didn't patronize your business early on want your services, charge them full price. Discounts belong to the ones who assisted you from the beginning. Your ride or die clients. I once took a class, and the business owner said, "Why should new clients get the benefits of what the old clients earned?" As your first guinea pigs, those people are to be cherished. After all, if I can't sell a free item, why would someone else pay for it. I have a childhood friend that endured all the horrible hairstyles I was terrible at. It took years for me to understand how to tame her hair. But throughout all of that craziness, she sent her family members and friends as paying clients. She also was on the same crew that showed up to support me in court for my son's custody case. What is essential to remember is that in life, it's so much easier to recycle through the same people for networking. Then you don't have to be embarrassed due to con games. Hearing from them is refreshing. This lady and I go gaps of time without talking, but whenever we connect again, it's like we never missed a beat. Each parting is filled with enough love to last until we see each other a year later.

I want to speak about family loyalty, particularly about the loyalty between husband and wife. Loyalty surpasses being in love by all accounts. It's a decision. It's a state of mind – a way of life. There were so many occasions where I was in the position of simply needing the presence of a person for support. I'm reminded of an occasion involving the geriatric sideshow I spoke of in the first chapter.

I remember waking up that morning having to go to court to fight her when she turned off the air conditioning. Umar went to work around 5 am. He turned back around to come home. When he walked in, I was confused. He explained that he felt that I needed him. The fact that a person loves you enough to take the time to read your spirit where you don't have to say a word is priceless. I did, in fact, need his support. He is the strongest person I know (both physically and mentally). So, whenever we have gone into unchartered territory, we both jump out of the proverbial plane together.

Remember when I said being an entrepreneur is similar to jumping out of a plane and building a parachute on the way down? Having a support system is like having a pilot, repair person, huge landing balloon, and jumping partner to make it a bit easier. Umar is my jumping partner. He's been studying his wife since day one.

Chapter 8
Defining Success

When I was a senior in high school, I remember announcing in bible study that I wanted to be a licensed cosmetologist. One of my neighbors was so excited for me and said what her vision for me was. She saw me as the owner of a big salon in the future. It took me years to say this, but that was not my goal.

My goal for cosmetology was very simple. I desired to just stand behind a chair. I loved the smell of marcel irons in a black hair salon. As a child, it touched my soul upon the entrance into the salons. I loved the eggy smell of the old school relaxers as it was being rinsed down the drain. I loved hearing the banging of bracelets as a hairstylist curled my hair. I loved the way I felt every time I left a hair salon with a new style. A big salon was not a goal for me at all, but that was where other people saw me in their dreams for me.

Once I began to work inside salons, I quickly realized how little desire I had to own a big salon. My vision for success was simply a salon suite by the time I was two years into the game. I remember the salon that I worked for when I graduated from hair school in 2000. It was beautiful. This owner had her salon laid out with beautiful furnishings. Behind the scenes, she was struggling. She was bouncing our paychecks left and right. The salon stylists banded together and left for a local salon suite concept location. There, everyone had their own room that was equipped with a shampoo bowl chair and hooded dryers. I didn't have a clientele at that point (mainly because I couldn't do hair), but my vision of having my dream met was to be able to afford to rent a space like that.

As I got older, I realized that other people's definitions of success didn't match my definition. I had two relatives mention that it isn't realistic to consider being a hairstylist as being a career. Soon after, my mother put it in perspective. She had me examine everyone who made such comments. I observed how their bi-weekly trips to the salon made a career for their stylists but, somehow, it wasn't reasonable for me to acquire that same career. Look at how every news anchor, public figure, and celebrity has their hair styled efficiently. Some contractors have made a career as a celebrity stylist or barber.

Success is relative. I took a class a few years ago. The teacher explained that if you had the desire to be the owner of a million-dollar business and your operations per minute could not produce that, then it would be unreasonable for you to have such a goal. For example, if one service took an hour and the most I could charge for that service was $400, how much per week could I make operating on an eight-hour daily schedule with no assistance? Her analysis made me reprioritize my vision for success. So, although my passion was to be a hairstylist, I always limited my schedule because otherwise, I will be burned out. When you are doing hair, and it becomes aggravating, thus feeling like an actual 9-5, it's clear it has to stop before the passion is gone. I also didn't want to deal with the stress of hiring contractors. When I did so for the first time, theft was a major issue. I didn't want the headache.

At one point, the irony of it all brought me to Everest College. I was studying to be a medical assistant in order to meet everyone else's vision of success. One of the same relatives, who I thought would be excited once I said I was now at Everest, now had a look of confusion. They didn't remember saying their opposition at all a decade earlier. That is when I realized that I am the one who dictates what my definition of success is. I came up with a game plan secretly and jumped out of the proverbial plane I keep referencing. I knew for certain it would be a hard sell to convince my husband to give me the starter funds, mainly because I was so indecisive about my goals. He is the reason I can sell you my product in 60 seconds. If I can't hold Umar's attention for 60 seconds in a business presentation, I can't hold anyone else's.

He gave me the $500, I purchased salon equipment, and that was the beginning of Mazyck Williams Enterprises. I was determined to push forward and hustle hard without relenting. There were so many times when both of us felt that this wasn't going to work. Then that day came when I knew I had officially sold Umar on this dream. He was working in the middle of nowhere in Virginia on a job site. Watch how this all ties together. Umar is the money saver, and I am the planner. So, I became the one who always made sure we had at least two running cars. He would at times not have his cars in good running condition. Once I started doing the house calls, I made the decision to always keep two cars. That way, if one car (out of three) broke down, we could both easily jump in a car and go to work without getting a rental.

This was one of those times. He left that morning and couldn't find his phone but needed a GPS to get to work. I always keep a spare phone by TracFone (remember, I'm the planner). I gave him my phone and he happened to be driving my spare car. On the way to work, the car started smoking. He got to work, my phone died, and he called me from a co-worker's line. He told me the circumstances and was about to drive the smoking car to our mechanic over 50 miles away. I stopped him, told him to give the address to me, and I'd handle it. When you work a 9-5 contract position, especially in blue-collar work, taking off is only an emergency option at times.

As he is saying the address, my phone is recording it (my business line records calls). I was in the middle of rinsing a relaxer from a client's hair at 6 am. There is no way I could have written that down without interrupting my client's service, as the client went under the dryer. I had already begun replaying the recording so I could get his address. Mind you, I keep a Bluetooth in my ear, so these business dealings are seamless. I adopted this Bluetooth system when I used to ride the train a lot, and having a toddler while on a call is nearly impossible without it at times. Within an hour, I:

1. Called AAA to schedule a pickup of the car.

2. Called the mechanic to schedule the arrival of the car.

3. Called Enterprise to arrange a pickup of the rental car.

4. Texted his co-worker back the details of the above arrangement.

5. Called the nursing home to tell them I'd be working a shortened schedule.

So, I was to go from Hyattsville to the boondocks somewhere in the sticks in Virginia by 2:30 pm.

The nursing home staff totally understood and were happy to accommodate me because I was an efficient contractor. I always showed up, I was polite to residents, and I always kept my word. So, I simply rescheduled all of the clients until the next day. When I arrived at 2:30 on the dot to pick Umar up, he was so happy. I will never forget him saying that he would never talk bad about my job again. That day officially cemented why I stopped talking bad about my own job as well and pushed forward relentlessly with this career choice.

Being an entrepreneur is like jumping out of an airplane and building a parachute on the way down. But the beauty is in the assistance you offer your team due to the flexibility in schedule. You see, I didn't have to ask a supervisor for permission. All I did was reschedule the contract for that day. I apologized to the relaxer client I was talking over, and she quickly excused the circumstances. Being an entrepreneur is the perfect career for family emergencies. If you have a client who doesn't understand, then that just ends that contract. You have 100 other mini contracts that aren't affected by that one client.

Success contingent depends on you taking yourself seriously. Do you have a website, business cards, discount cards, or visibility on social media platforms? These platforms contribute to the thriving of your business. The business isn't a physical location, it is an extension of you. You set the rules and expectations for your business, so if it fails, you are to blame. That is why you have to be relentless. Even when it feels like it's failing, always remember that the business isn't the physical space but the entity itself. Now we have websites. Virtual business platforms changed the way we define business forever.

Another aspect of flexibility is if you have children or are caring for a disabled or elderly relative. There have been countless occasions in which a flexible schedule was necessary for peace of mind, as it relates to the four of us as a family unit. When we moved to a different county, we encountered an enormous amount of problems with the local school system. It got so out of control, I was forced to seek assistance from numerous state and federal agencies. There were many moments when I had to change my work schedule. I needed to physically be there in the mornings for my children because, in all honesty, many people were crazy and unpredictable. The key factor was the fact that my schedule was unpredictable. So, while other parents had restricted schedules, the school district had no idea when and where I would pop up. There were many days in which I would cancel an entire schedule to be there for my children. Having a 9-5 does not afford that luxury.

My initial reason at the age of 9 or 10 years old for deciding to become an entrepreneur was the fact that my parents worked 9-5 schedules. I remember how they would talk about how crazy their supervisors were. I asked my dad one day what it meant if you don't have a boss. He told me: "That means you're an entrepreneur. You are your own boss." That was the deciding factor for me, and by 11, I knew cosmetology was the avenue that would open the doors. Success, in my eyes, resonated with simply the title alone: an entrepreneur.

Chapter 9
Charging

We sometimes don't know our value. By we, I mostly mean me. Charging didn't come into perspective until I thought of the make-up analogy I spoke of in an earlier chapter. I started thinking of all the things we use as a family that are a price that I don't charge, such as when we went to the Baltimore Aquarium, as I spoke of previously. How about the new car we purchased? Did the dealer care whether or not the bank financed it, or you had a check? Absolutely not. If you didn't qualify for the loan, that is a personal problem. They will simply market to the next consumer who doesn't share your financial problems. How about your accountant for tax season? Does it matter to him that you had to borrow that $300 fee from your cousin? Absolutely not. It only matters that the check cleared.

I found myself at a critical moment of self-reflection while purchasing a $200 bag for the following reasons:

1. It had my two brands on it.

2. I needed a professional-looking bag for house calls when I serviced clients at their homes.

So, although I am not the type of person who would ever pay $200 for someone else's brand, I found myself understanding my brand's value. I provided a spectacular service. I always showed up unless it was an emergency. I was polite to clients. I just wanted to have attire and a bag to match the experience I was giving my clients – like the way they felt when a cable guy or electrician came to their house, not the kitchen stylist who just rolled out of the bed. I wanted them to understand that the $100 they were about to give me was for a $100 experience. With that being said, this goes hand in hand with phone calls. It is important to understand that you must not be on the phone the entire time your client is being serviced. They want to feel special.

Sometimes, efficiency comes after dealing with a difficult client. It's amazing that an altercation with a client resulted in me utilizing an online system that made my talk time disappear. This client kept forgetting appointments. I still use this appointment software to this very day. At the time, I was overworking my brain by manually putting appointments into another manual calendar. That client was also quite demanding of time. In my world, you cannot have both. If you are a forgetter, I don't give you early or dedicated appointments if I haven't yet fired you. Yes, I fire clients. If you are demanding, you get dedicated appointments because I know you're actually coming. It's common sense. So, you can't get a priority appointment during prime time then not show up and expect I'll keep giving you those appointments just because you ask. I place you into a category. You must pay a deposit and schedule online. She was the first one I forced to schedule online. That was so that the system sent a reminder, and the client made the appointment themselves. This alleviated the "I forgot" premise because it now becomes the client's problem.

After I did that, I realized that I now had to manually input all of my client's information into the new database. I then gave power to my clients to now be able to set appointments without me being the middleman. That was so freeing. I was now able to put my phone on silent after 4 pm for clients. If they needed to speak to me, it now had to be during business hours. This gave me time to spend with my family and to improve my business even more. You must be able to turn off the business during specific times. That can be hard, so I've come to the point where I shut down the phone call aspect of it. I paid for a service that issues auto-replies. Even email service providers have that feature with emails. Certain social media outlets for business provide similar services as well.

These automated means of communications help small businesses a great deal! You may not have the income initially so that $25 a month for text reminders for appointments helps you stay on top of things efficiently. Think of what you would have to pay an actual person. The software even has a feature where an actual operator can answer your calls for a monthly fee!

This increases your value as a small business. When you receive an automated reminder from your cable provider when the technician is on the way, it gives an air of professionalism. When you visit a website that is color-coordinated, you feel a certain way. So, if you walk into a store that's decked out, where everyone is dressed up, violins are playing, and complimentary snacks are in treat bags, you expect to pay more than if you walked into a hole in the wall. How many holes in walls have you walked into and just known that you were not going to be charged market rate because it looked so bad in and around the establishment?

Well, that is how it was when I worked at a salon prior to the birth of my first son. It was the definition of a hole in the wall:

1. Snake in the bathroom (yes, read that again).

2. Flies.

3. Faulty air conditioning.

4. Roaches.

5. Mice.

6. A man who repeatedly pleasured himself at the front window at random.

7. Plumbing problems.

8.   Dirty parking lot.

By the time I was six months in, my clients stopped coming. Not to mention the fact that my co-workers and I would smoke weed between clients – that smell follows you. I would also show up chronically late. I still had clients, but my ability to grow and increase clientele was stomped out. The package I was presenting was horrible.

That ridiculousness got much worse once my eldest son's father came home from a stint in prison. We grew up together, and this man kept an old business card in his wallet over the years, and my number did not change. At the time, I was a straight-up "sucka" as my husband would say. I didn't know how to put up boundaries at all, nor did I have an understanding of how to defend myself psychologically.

Before I knew it, this guy was driving my brand-new car. He would drop me off at work, ride around in my car, and return it to me empty. I wouldn't say a word. I pretended it didn't bother me. His presence in conjunction with the array of people I was surrounded by was toxic. It is no environment for an entrepreneur to thrive in. One of the people in my circle even stole an ATM card from me to get gas. I knew it was her because the location of the transaction on the statement was near her house.

Before I knew it, I was pregnant with my son. I had lost my grips on reality, my clients, my apartment, and all of those alleged friends. I was alone. When he was born, I was a complete mess. He ended up in foster care for a few months. His paternal grandparents were of great assistance to me at the worst time of my life. Not one family member reached out to assist me. From one perspective, I can't blame them. I was a mess. But from another perspective, I didn't understand because everyone falls from time to time. I was only 24. Looking back, I'm glad they didn't. All of those experiences molded me. They actually hardened me and prepared me for motherhood, entrepreneurship, as well as fighting white supremacy.

The label of "white supremacy" is not explained thoroughly. What I came to realize is that many white people don't even know how to battle let alone dismantle white supremacy. That's why we see these movements in packs. White supremacy, in itself, is a form of bullying. So, as I spoke of the business owner who was a slumlord, most people assumed it was white owners. The sad fact is that once black people have reached the pinnacle of what they view as valuable, they adopt the same measures that stood in the way of our ancestors. The deeper question is, if our culture was erased, then how could we not adopt the image of value that this society puts on themselves?

Moving to a different side of town made me understand that the white children and parents who decided to join in terrorizing our family did so for one of the three reasons:

1. They were scared of being ostracized for not participating.

2. They fell for lies through the whisper campaigns that were launched.

3. They were just flat out racist or had criminal skeletons they needed hidden.

There were only a select few that met the third reason – the rest were just going along with it. I realized that they valued not being ostracized, similar to what I had known growing up around black people. The primary difference is the lengths they would go to conceal each other's criminal activity. They moved like a pack of savage wolves, blackmailing whomever they needed to in the process. We, as black folk (where I'm from), could see a lawsuit coming a mile away and quickly covered our behinds before state and federal agencies became involved.

The white side of things ran deep. The way they knew each other in high-up positions was unbelievable. The difference between now and 50-100 years ago was the fact that all these educated black folks that migrated from the South settled in the D.M.V. (D.C., Maryland, and Virginia) area. So now, those generations of brown people have positions up in government agencies. You must keep in mind that the white people in that area close to D.C. are more liberal, or at least they hide the racism better.

How can black people expect an answer from white people on how to stop white supremacy when white people can't stop it? They bully each other. Sure, that's not defined as white supremacy by Webster, but it is bullying. After I spoke with multiple parents in my town, I quickly came to realize that the major players who terrorized families also terrorized other white families. Some of these people were treated horribly. That is why once the federal investigation ended, although the district made clear changes to policy, the results came back unfounded. How can they say my children were treated differently when they treated the other families who were white in a similar way? Thus, the county-wide change in policy. It was difficult to prove the racism aspect as the sole reason for treatment because they treated each other in nasty ways as well. This was truly eye-opening.

Everything made perfect sense once I found another family online whose children experienced similar things that my children did. This mother was aggressive. She made a website exposing the whole county! All the skeletons were on this site! I was screaming in the house when I found her site. This was when I realized that each and every time I had a meeting with the board of education, my children would be physically attacked. What they didn't expect is that my kids can fight. It was like clockwork. I soon came to realize that the principal had mastered a loophole in legalities. If you don't instruct someone directly to attack someone, it's not illegal. So, she was the head of a whisper campaign that came to a head after I located this lady's website. The superintendent, board, police, bus contractors, teacher, and students were all entangled in this circus. Watch how this comes together. I had previously:

1. Battled certain family members psychologically.

2. Battled my son's grandparents in court.

3. Battled that psychopathic geriatric landlord in chapter 1.

4. Battled that supervisor who was micromanaging.

5. Battled that last slumlord.

I would not have been able to battle the mob of townspeople who were involved in concealing the disgusting cesspool of drama if I had not had these prior experiences.

I only found out it was the principal who launched the whisper campaign because she is the one who filed the fraudulent restraining order. Yes, you read that right. This chick put all her lies in writing. Just like how my son's grandparents did for the custody hearing. The difference was the fact that this time, I was prepared. You see because my family testified against me in court during the custody trial, I now knew for certain that I could sit perfectly still in a fit of rage without speaking or reacting. Because I watched blatant lies ejaculate from said family members' mouths during the same trial, I knew I could take that without screaming. So, once I arrived at court, we were pulling case law in the hallway. Had I not had to research case law in my son's custody hearing, I would have never known how to use it without an attorney in a U.S. court of law. Had I not met my husband, I never would have known how to properly and effectively use said case law. Had he never been incarcerated, he wouldn't have been able to advise me about legal matters and how this court system works. I battled my own people for years prior to that moment. White supremacy was a direct mirror of the black supremacy my own kinfolk had inflicted on me years prior. My skin folk had adopted the very thing we marched against – bullying.

So, as I'm in court walking in with golden brown skin (and had a hijab too), this principal was a nervous wreck. Manipulators are weak because they only thrive from explosive reactions. As my reaction was to sit still and not yell, it rendered the principal and all her hostages helpless. Let me explain what I meant by hostages. Do you know that lady got at least 20 staff members to accompany her to court the day before Christmas Eve? If my supervisor asked me to come to court for a restraining order, I would not come. Their paychecks and pensions were the hostages should they have declined.

Going back a few days prior, the mother I spoke of earlier, who was fighting the school system, was aggressive. She was in numerous local newspapers as well. She was in litigation with the school system. From the way her daughter was treated, I assumed it was a black family. When I found out these were white people standing up for black people (they objected to the wide use of the n-word in the school system), I was shocked. I thought everyone in the town was the same. She was different. She was even more beautiful than them as well, which explained the jealousy people had towards her. This lady showed up to a board hearing with me. When I walked up to her, I immediately knew who she was. She was so soft-spoken I was amazed. This lady was fighting for her kids as aggressively as I was. I found out about pedophilia documented in the school system. I found out about many secrets that I wasn't looking for. I used that leverage to demand relief for my children. I sent a "happy holidays" email after the board of education president refused to help me. It had a link to the website of the mother they were fighting. These people had multiple conniptions. I found their secret, and that was powerful leverage to force them to intervene with the bullying inflicted upon my children.

Soon after, I made my own site and launched it. I made sure not to tell either child. I only told adults, including the principal and her minions. So how was it that the next day, all the kids knew about the site? That proved that adults were telling kids adult business. I grew up knowing to stay out of adult discussions. My son had a day of peace right after that. The following day, the principal filed all her lies in court as a last-ditch effort to force a volatile reaction. My reaction had to match the monster she painted me as in her whisper campaigns. The judge ended up granting half of the order. I was allowed to go to the school, but I couldn't contact her, which was fine with me. The ridiculous part about it was I tried to not contact her at the beginning of the school year, and the district literally forced me to recommence contact with her. My children were being physically assaulted 5-10 times monthly. No protection was afforded then, and when they began to defend themselves, the district allowed the principal to initiate actual charges against my son (which were dropped). Everyone seemed scared to confront this lady.

The way we as people of all backgrounds value ourselves is based on who we are surrounded by as well. Is your circle of people steering you toward your best? Are they steering you toward staying within legalities? How are their finances? If you work for bullies or your life is surrounded by chaos, it affects what you can charge. This is the importance of facing problems head-on as they come. The aftermath of not battling is detrimental to your mental health, which is necessary for the entrepreneur.

Chapter 10

Health and Entrepreneurship

When I turned 30, my body changed. For some reason, I couldn't eat what I used to. Well, I could technically eat it, but I would suffer the consequences. One day, I had a sandwich from a fast-food restaurant and was violently throwing up. I had to cancel a whole book of clients on a Saturday. I remember being home and not being able to move. All of a sudden, Umar burst in the room saying something to the effect of "Your body has rights over you! You're an old hag now. You can't keep eating this bull&*it." I couldn't even crack back on him for the old hag comment due to the pain. All I could do is sit there curled up in the fetal position as he took the children out to give me peace. I didn't realize it until he said something, but I was experiencing this once a year. At that time, I was pushing 35. I decided to attempt to eat only halal meats. I noticed an immediate difference. All of a sudden, I had the energy to actually cook every day. Prior to that, I was so drained that cooking an actual meal from scratch was nearly impossible.

This was affecting my work life as well. If your health isn't good, you can't function efficiently. I noticed over the years, as I started weeding out certain things, I was able to function more efficiently. It changes your thought process. More recently, I decided to change from deodorant to mineral salt. I noticed another spike in energy. This time, I had the energy to begin to exercise. Although it is far from regular, it is more than what it was some years ago. I noticed that change coincided with a change in my ability to control my temperament better than what it had been before.

Your environment can also change your ability to control your anger. I remember there were many incidents and altercations when I worked as a contractor inside the nursing home. One day, a resident had a violent temper tantrum. This lady did have a sweet side, but this day was not one of the days she was displaying it. She was ripping the shampoo cape off while I was simultaneously attempting to put it on. I had two outside clients in the room, as well as the resident's great-granddaughter and daughter. As she was throwing the violent tantrum, I remained calm and still knew I had about ten minutes to execute this hairstyle. All of a sudden, the family started arguing once the nurse entered the room. It was a scene from a reality show. I literally blocked them out of my mind because I was down to five minutes before this patient had a meltdown. I proceeded to duck and dodge her as she was literally throwing punches and clawing to draw blood. I blew dry it, threw four plats in it, and it was over. I was ready for the next client. The outside clients stood in amazement. I didn't break a sweat.

Being in volatile environments contributed to the patience necessary to maintain good health. Being in a constant state of anger is detrimental to your health. There is an article by Harvard published in 2011 that states, "Chronic anger and anxiety can disrupt cardiac function by changing the heart's electrical stability, hastening atherosclerosis, and increasing systemic inflammation" (source: https://www.hsph.harvard.edu/news/magazine/happiness-stress-heart-disease/). So, although I didn't understand it then, working at the nursing home was a boot camp for anger control. Each client was a ticking time bomb. There were many circumstances out of my control. When dealing with dementia patients, their actions are as unpredictable as a toddler at times.

One day, I was servicing a client who I had been for a number of years. She had never snapped on me until I was almost a decade into doing her hair. One day, she came in and said for me to not dye her hair grey again like I did the last time. I was stuck. How could I convince this lady that she was already grey for years? The dementia had her believing she was a young woman, and her hair was black. I was in my head the whole time contemplating how I was not going to show her the mirror to prevent an altercation. Boy oh boy, when she got a glimpse, she snapped! I tried to hold in my laugh. I couldn't finish. I had to take her upstairs because she was cursing so bad. She then took it a step further and proceeded to spit on me. Well, she attempted to. She was pushing 90 so I ducked quickly. Plus, her saliva glands didn't seem to work well either. She was spitting out pretend spit. If that isn't anger management, I don't know what is. It also assists greatly in maintaining a straight face.

There were countless occasions where maintaining my anger was necessary, such as:

1. When a client stripped naked in the hall, shouting as we passed.

2. When the business office was siphoning money out of patients' accounts and blaming it on me, although I had no direct access to patient funds.

3. When another administrator attempted to micromanage me, although I was an independent contractor.

4. When the building had to be quarantined multiple times prior to covid, leaving me out of work for weeks,

5. When a patient's husband tried to get me to fraudulently notarize a document for an unconscious resident.

These (and many more) incidents helped me to prioritize life into two categories. The first being if I should invest time in getting upset, and the second being if I should let it go. After all, stress and anger will literally kill you. You'll die at your own hands. I found that 95-99% of things were not worth the time it took to care about the issue, let alone get angry. I walked around with liability protection on my mind, period. For example, when I had a psychopathic person adamant about retrieving a volatile reaction from me, I simply documented things and mastered formulating a jugular email. My emails will take your breath away, especially if you're a lying manipulator. They (lying manipulators) are so stupid that if you sit still long enough, they think they're smarter than you and dig their own grave.

Let me take you back to 2017 for this example. I was battling all three of my son's family members involved in the custody battle. It was ridiculous. On one hand, if we had an upcoming court date, the father would be the father of the year, posting photos on social media and such things. At this particular time, he hadn't seen the kid in months (but the grandparents were still getting him), but on court day, he was brought into the hearing on closed-circuit TV. I almost passed out when they turned the TV on, and he was on the screen. I was thinking how can he show up on this but skip visitations? They had a good game. The grandparents were faithful. They always came to get the child. But after a while, when he said he didn't want to go, I got tired of forcing him. He kept telling me these horror stories during the visitations. I put all of them in the court motion for response to contempt they accused me of once I refused to meet them any longer.

The most ridiculous part was that my lawyer made the court order so smooth, they refused to abide by it. They were supposed to pick the kid up on Friday evening directly from the school then drop him back off at the school Monday morning. They unofficially switched it to cater to their schedule (although the grandmother wasn't working and had the most flexible schedule). After a certain time, I got tired of altering my work schedule to drop off the kid at a police station so they could be accommodated. Especially for a couple that, after they helped me, were behaving almost like psychos in our town. They were vicious with the whisper campaigns. They had mastered it. They had people believing that the true description of who their son was actually describing me. When I read the first rebuttal, I was thinking that they sounded like they were describing their son! They even lied and said I sporadically visited the child. I was there weekly (only twice at that) because the grandmother restricted the schedule to fit the future narrative they spun to all their gullible minions. A bit like white supremacy.

Anyway, I just got the first salon location. They served me there. I didn't know what to do, but since I was fighting that geriatric freak show of a landlord, their notice didn't pale in comparison. One month prior to the hearing, I was searching online as I always did to stay alert on drama to use against them in court. Boy oh boy! I stumbled upon fresh restraining orders. These were final, meaning that sufficient proof was given to receive such protections. I was so excited I was in tears. I was screaming. I couldn't tell the kid because it wasn't necessary for him to know. Plus, children don't know what to do with certain information. They run their mouths too much. It's best to put them out of the room when discussing such matters.

Soon after, Umar and I drove down to the courthouse. They have limited information online, so I had to physically go down to see who sought out restraining orders. Umar had to sit in the car. When I got in there, I saw it was the grandparents who got the restraining order against (get this) their son! I was in tears from overwhelming joy. The irony of the situation was none other than what was written by Allah. He is the best of planners. Hunny darling sweetie pie! It said he allegedly ripped the screen door off of their house and was acting a fool. He allegedly threatened them with alleged gang violence and more! (HUNNY BAYBAYYYYY!!!!)

See, these grandparents could have very well have been lying. If they lied to my face under oath, who am I to say they were telling the truth. I wasn't there. But who cares! That's why I like certain aspects of the alleged justice system in the United

States. They change the definition of the truth. They consider the truth whatever you say your truth is! They spent years in court documents stating how their son had "turned his life around" and was an upstanding dad. I think it was embarrassing for them to admit it wasn't true. When the grandmother used to talk with me prior to the custody battle, she voiced her opinion about her embarrassment. Anyway, everything that I said in my rebuttal to the visitation motion that they said I lied about was confirmed in their restraining order. When I called the attorney, she said I didn't even need her anymore. She told me to write down what to say and sent me to court alone.

I stood there as the grandfather ejaculated his predictable lies out of his mouth, even stating they hadn't seen the kid anytime recently when he just came up to the school to see the child months prior. That judge looked at me and asked why I was denying visitation. I started out by saying that their house isn't suitable for an adult, let alone a child, that they have three different restraining orders against their junkie son currently, and he ripped the screen door off of the house. I went on and on until the judge turned red. He literally turned red. The grandfather was stuck looking like a mannequin. It was a scene from a reality show. I am still laughing right now as I'm typing this! The judge postponed the case until they could secure a new attorney. He said my attorney had to be present next time.

The next hearing was basically stating to all parties that we were in limbo. See, now the grandparents couldn't be a united front against me by joining arms with their son because of the restraining orders. If they were lying about the circumstances surrounding the restraining orders (which I am almost certain they were), they now had to convince a judge which lie they were sticking with. To add insult to injury, the kid was getting older. The court order was simply a sheet of paper. Soon, he would be a teenager and come and go as he pleased. They literally taught us this in the court-ordered parenting class. A child can't be tricked forever. So, no matter what lies they told my son, my spirit made him gravitate to me like a magnet. Just like my clients. It's magnetic when your spirit is sweet.

So now, even if the grandparents wanted to move forward, they would have to overcome a serious hurdle. They have to serve all parties involved. If they allegedly cut ties with their son, then they can't verify they know where he lives in order to serve him. It was like watching the catch-22 of all catch-22s. I was speechless. After a while, I started taking him to the grandparents' house once I was certain the father wasn't there. I took him when he desired to go, which wasn't as often as the order demanded. Kids grow up. They also hate court. I took him until he was able to understand for himself how to articulate if he did or didn't want to go and why. It just validated all the body language I was reading all those years, but he couldn't properly articulate it as a younger child.

All of that was anger control boot camp. Pretending that stuff didn't bother me tricked my mind into believing it didn't bother me until Allah shut the whole thing down.

Chapter 11

Dawn and Umar

My life was a hot mess when I met Umar. So, let me take you back. I had my eldest in April of 2006. Umar was just being released from prison around the same time. I kept meeting different guys, but when I met Umar, he was a grown man. I mean a grown man. When I say a grown man, I mean he knew what he wanted. He knew he wanted a wife, how she would talk, how she would raise his future son. He wanted a son. I remember him saying, "I'm not saying I'll be perfect, but I am who I say I am." I never heard anyone say my name like he did. I never heard anyone talk like he did. I never in my life met anyone with a poker face like he had. I never met anyone who was as aggressive as he was. I never met anyone who was as strong mentally as he was. I also had never been up and close to a Muslim before.

He was always praying. Like all the time. I remember just watching him in awe. It was indescribable. He had a support system that a billionaire had. Not money. He just never wanted for anything, and I mean anything. I never saw anything like it. If his car broke down, someone would let him borrow theirs. If he needed clothes, someone would give them to him. He kept a job like it was nothing. I watched so many ex-offenders say they couldn't get work, and yet this man had two jobs and a new car less than a year out of prison? I knew, whatever he had as a blessing system, I wanted it. I was attracted to Islam because of the structure. Like I said, I was a mess. I wasn't raising my son. I was the definition of a deadbeat. I couldn't provide for my son.

All I was doing was visiting him. One day, he told me, "When your son grows up, he is going to cuss you out!" I was brought to tears as I wondered why. He said it was because I wasn't trying hard enough. He was right. I was a mess.

One thing I admired about Umar was the fact that he was sober. Because I was always around weed heads, I didn't understand how it was even possible. When we met in February 2007, it was because my apartment was the party apartment. His nephew had already been there with a neighbor of mine a day or so prior. One day, Umar gave him a ride to my apartment after his nephew was telling him there were ladies there. Umar came in all quiet with his straight face. I was talking my ridiculous trash because someone lied to me and told me he said something about me. I was all up in his face then stepped off. His nephew came into my room and asked who I was and how old I was. Before he got to the third question, I demanded to know why he wanted to know these things. He said that his uncle liked me. I asked why he didn't ask himself, and he said, that he was shy. I gave the nephew my number, and Umar called me from the car. It was snowing. He called me and asked if I would come outside, and I declined. We talked for three months or so over the phone. We ended up going on our first date because another nephew wanted his hair done so Umar paid for him to get it done. We went to Chinatown in D.C. to see a movie.

Soon after, my apartments suddenly started to get vandalized. I can't say who did it, but what I will say is that two other ladies whose apartments were vandalized after parting ways with my eldest son's dad. So, let's just say I don't believe in coincidences. Before I knew it, Umar's uncle allowed me to stay with him at his house in D.C. We stayed there for years. It was necessary for the healing of my mind. The family structure taught me about loyalty, and to set emotion aside for the greater good.

The way Allah wrote for us to cross paths was beautiful. We had a son in 2008 and were married soon after. We eloped.

I remember his uncle fussing at us saying, "You can't do this! You have to tell people you're getting married!" But we were in love, so that was irrelevant. He ended up going with us to the mosque that evening. He held our son during a later part of the ceremony. I remember, as I said our vows, I was holding the baby. It was a day I'll never forget. I spent a year trying to decide if I should take Shahada prior to this day. I knew that if we had a child, I would definitely convert to avoid confusing the child. Becoming Muslim was an executive decision. I was the CEO of my body, and I needed the structure. I needed the defined rules to be efficient. I needed the motivation of a husband who tells the truth no matter how much it hurts. That verbal motivation is essential for the soul.

After the birth of my eldest son, I had many horrible moments. After I met Umar, he was there for all of them. It is monumental to have somebody that would drop everything for you, spend his last dime on you, and risk his life for you. That is the true definition of a friend. Who can say that? A man who met you at your rock bottom, assisting you for the reward of Allah when everyone else ran away. He is the definition of battle mode – that mode is essential for the thriving of business.

After all those years of battling, what I realized was that I kept facing the same demon in a different body over and over again. I was getting proficient at running. One day, my husband told me: "If the same thing keeps happening over and over again, did you ever think it might be you?" Allah kept making sure I encountered these psychos so I'd master how to defeat them. It was like reliving the same day over and over for years. What I learned is that the Shayteen (or Satan as some refer to him) is not efficient. People who use evil methods know how to disguise patterns for intellect. Intellectual beings can come up with countless creative ideas at a moment's notice.

Lying manipulators are predictable and easy to stop. They can't control their anger. They also make it clear to who they are spreading whisper campaigns. It is extremely predictable. If you sit still and play dumb, they tell on themselves. They think everyone is less intelligent than them, or at least that is the lie they tell themselves. Practice straight faces, don't be too friendly initially, set boundaries, and study people. Manipulators didn't just start with you. They've been perfecting their lies for years, simultaneously studying people's reactions and gauging which lie they should tell next. The thing about lies you must remember is that all lies have an expiration date.

Like I told my son when he was scared to fight mentally, once you realize that every day you have to fight, your perspective will change. You will be prepared to fight if your mindset changes. Being an entrepreneur is the ultimate fight. It's YOU versus the better version of you. Now let's get this money.

www.ingramcontent.com/pod-product-compliance
Lightning Source LLC
Chambersburg PA
CBHW030357280726